Kayak & Canoe
Games

Laurie Gullion

Illustrations by Les Fry

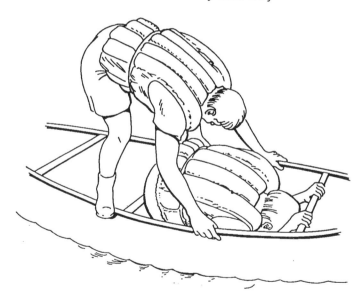

Menasha Ridge Press
Birmingham, Alabama

American Canoe Association
Springfield, Virginia

Acknowledgements

Many ideas in this book come from teaching with veteran instructors at the Outdoor Center of New England. Special thanks go to Jim Abel, Tom Foster, Dick Irving, David Su, Michael Lyle, and Jill Runnion for the years spent keeping the fun in paddling programs.

I'd like to thank Peter Kennedy at Adventure Quest in Vermont and Claudia Kerckhoff-Van Wijk at Madawaska Kanu Camp in Ontario for sharing written material developed in their paddling programs for kids.

Thanks also to the following people for sharing ideas about youth programs: Syl Mathis, St. Alban's School/ National Cathedral School Voyageur Program; Wayne Dickert, Nantahala Outdoor Center; Heidi Krantz, Umiak Outfitters.

Budd Zehmer's good humor at Menasha was greatly appreciated.

Thanks to these ACA staff and members who offered helpful feedback: Jeff Buchman, Deborah Macmillan, Sue Plankis, and Charlie Wilson.

And endless gratitude to my husband, Bruce Lindwall, who survived another manuscript.

© 1996 by The American Canoe Association

Printed in the United States of America
Published by Menasha Ridge Press
First edition, first printing

Illustrations by Les Fry
Text design and production
by Carolina Graphics Group

American Canoe Association
7432 Alban Station Boulevard, Suite B-226
Springfield, Virginia 22150

Menasha Ridge Press
700 South 28th Street
Birmingham, Alabama 35233

Contents

Playing Games With Paddling

Young and old want to have fun outdoors, and they are more likely to paddle again if they meet this goal. Learning how to paddle is effective when it's enjoyable and it serves as the means to satisfy a goal—like a child's desire to race past another boat or an adult's interest in enjoying an outing with a partner!

Lighthearted paddling games can encourage relaxed, efficient skill development at any age and at any ability. The purpose of this guide is to enhance the enjoyment and safety of canoeists and kayakers through interesting activities that build solid skills and knowledge.

I've been building a bag of tricks for twenty years. My love for paddling games started at Linden Hill School in Northfield, Massachusetts, a residential school for dyslexic boys. My husband, who is also a teacher, and I often led recreational trips that began with an instructional session.

These kids, who learn best through a multisensory approach, taught me to adapt my more technical teaching style to their needs. And I discovered that it also worked with adults in other paddling programs. Forget boring technical explanations!

These new paddlers responded incredibly well to a method that involves lots of light-hearted doing—hearing, seeing, and feeling an activity simultaneously. When I began to use fun games like Spin City and Wet Sponge Polo, I realized their paddling skills developed quickly without a moment of restlessness.

Using a games approach also encourages the safe development of young paddlers, some of whom are inherent thrillseekers. Engaging activities on flatwater and at moving water practice sites keeps them interested, builds good skills, and helps to prevent too fast a transition to challenging whitewater.

The activities in this book are designed to give you a foundation for creating your own water playground. Parents, teachers, and camp counselors already have the resources to create a wealth of games beyond the ideas here. Use your imagination to create endless variations, and enjoy the unlimited possibilities for getting everyone excited about this sport.

Lively Instruction

Just where is the learning? That's what some observers watching the antics of water tag might ask. Improvement in paddling skills is happening right before their eyes, but it may be so informal that it bears little resemblance to a lesson.

Forget lengthy technical explanations!

How does this approach work? Sometimes I use the activities for practice after introducing a technical tip, because lots of relaxed practice is encouraged. At other times I sneakily replace the technical instruction with a game that targets a specific skill, and afterward I bring what they've learned to the group's attention.

The activities in this resource guide fit into the lesson framework endorsed by the American Canoe Association (ACA):

1. On land orientation
2. Calm water practice
3. Moving water practice

This handbook is designed to supplement the ACA's *Canoeing and Kayaking Instruction Manual* and *Introduction to Paddling,* where leaders will find the basic technical content necessary for instruction. Please refer to these manuals for more intensive review of technical information if you need it.

No attempt has been made to identify games for whitewater. Most instructors find that whitewater provides plenty of engaging action, so few games are needed!

Ready for action? Let's go!

Safe and Enjoyable Play

Boundaries

Set appropriate physical boundaries for each activity with buoys or available objects (like boulders, docks, ledge outcroppings). I often use a rectangular area of 25 yards by 50 yards—about one-quarter of a football field—for about 10 boats. A larger playing area is needed as paddling abilities improve or boat numbers increase. In some cases, a rectangular game area needs clear water between it and the shore, so people can glide past the boundaries marked by buoys if they can't stop easily.

Establish clear behavioral guidelines for all activities.

Any activities that require running entries into boats need a safe, sloping, obstacle-free shoreline. Be aware of such obstacles as docks, rafts, and moored boats, and use them wisely.

Beyond the physical boundaries, establish clear behavioral guidelines for activities to encourage safe play. Monitor the action appropriately to ensure that the participants observe the rules. Rescue by the individual and the group must make rescue a priority. Everyone needs to understand his or her responsibilities for safe paddling, and games can encourage and develop this safety awareness.

Collisions

Activities that encourage high-speed collisions of boats and paddles can be unsafe and should be avoided. Instead, choose activities that encourage the use of open space. With some groups, hand passing of balls, sponges, or other props can be safer than paddle passes or whacks. Establish what constitutes a "tag": a paddle touch to a boat (not a body), or a ball touch to a body or boat. Ball tags at shoulder-level or below are best.

Some games have an inevitable clashing of paddles and boats that is part of the action. Modifying game rules can help to prevent problems, where striking another player's paddle is a foul, and possession goes to the other team for a shot on the goal. With some, playing a game without paddles is the safest strategy. What's more, they may find that hand paddling in kayaks can be great fun.

Avoid asking paddlers to converge at a central spot if their ability or willingness to stop is marginal!

Controlled Capsizing

Capsizing is inevitable, so it provides players with excellent rescue practice. If paddlers are likely to tip over, adequate water depth for safe capsizing is important. Of course, the wearing of life jackets is essential.

Be aware that initial paddling comfort is often proportional to swimming ability, and non-swimmers may be uncomfortable with more hectic activities. However, my experience is that they become much more relaxed once they experience controlled capsizing.

Supply the group with clear guidelines for how to handle an overturned boat within a game. Where rolling ability is limited, the leader may decide that all action must stop until the paddler is upright. With experienced boaters who have good rolls, a leader may introduce a rule that a rolling player immediately be given five feet of clearance on all sides. Interference with rolling may provoke a penalty of some kind.

Role of Leader

Know your objectives. Leaders with limited control over their groups often have ill-defined objectives. Having fun is an important goal, but it has to be accompanied by more specific objectives targeted to key paddling skills to be effective for learning.

Be part of the action. Rather than directing from shore, be one of the players. Your paddling can provide an excellent model, and your enthusiasm for the sport will be contagious. What's more, kids love seeing you involved. A whistle is an effective tool to stop play and is more likely to be heard from within the game than from shore.

Be flexible, and change the guidelines where necessary to increase safety and to enhance enjoyment. Be ready to stop the action immediately if you sense the energy is spinning out of control. A "freeze" or "time out" signal understood by all is essential.

Be flexible: change the guidelines when necessary

Leadership shouldn't always remain with the adult leader. The best games emphasize three ingredients: fun, participation, and empowerment. Even young kids are capable of being good mini-leaders, directing the action, and deciding the rules (with supervision). Incorporate participants, and they'll have a vested interest in the activity.

Total Participation

The best games keep everyone playing, especially the slower or less-skilled paddlers. Avoid elimination games, which put the people who most need the practice on the sidelines. If some paddlers need rest breaks, they can become "props" or obstacles used by other boats.

Structure activities so that they don't always favor the fast or strongest paddlers. Select activities like a freestyle water ballet that requires finesse or canoe orienteering that requires other skills like map reading.

Choosing Teams

People generally know who paddles well and who doesn't. The leader should choose fair teams and avoid the nasty consequences of letting team captains pick their teammates. A mix of abilities can be important, while other games benefit from dividing teams by skill levels. All in all, change the teams often to avoid creating cliques.

Here are some quick ways to divide groups:

- By color—"All green boats here...find a partner wearing your colors..."
- By favorites—"Beatles fans here....Rolling Stones fans there..."
- By quick tricks—"Hold up a hand, right-handers over here..."
- By birthdays—"January to June over here...."

Intensity and Duration

Match the intensity of the activity to the players' paddling abilities and physical conditioning. Games can be energy-intensive, so be willing to end an activity when people might be tired. Call a time out when players need to breathe!

Don't beat a good game into the ground. Stop it when interest and energy is high. Then players will want to return to the game at another time.

Remember your age group. Youngsters (seven- and eight-year-olds) have a short attention span and can get fatigued, so even a half-day program can be too long.

Competition vs. Cooperation

Competitive games like relay races and head-to-head paddling can be an important tool in a program which is developing young racers. Beating other paddlers or racing against a timeclock can provide important motivation for improving skills.

Generally, recreation programs are most effective for the majority when they emphasize cooperative games or "Personal Best" achievement. For instance, establish a 2-point course over 30 yards, and ask paddlers to count the number of strokes taken to reach the farthest point. Then, on the return trip, ask each person to reduce the number of strokes, by focusing on one element of technique. You supply the focus, and each paddler can keep working to reduce the number of strokes. There is no need to compare final numbers.

Basic Safety Checklist

Always equip your group with the proper equipment, including safety gear. Make sure all boats and equipment are in good repair, because beginners are likely to bring their hands, arms, and legs into contact with them.

- Smooth gunwales and cockpits
- No interior/exterior sharp edges or points
- Adequate end lines on canoes (long and thick enough for effective rescues)
- Reinforced front and back decks on kayaks (float bags or foam panels)
- Blunt ends on boats for large group games
- Safety gear appropriate to the environment and activity
- Soft props and soft balls for tag games
- Life jackets
- Throw bags
- Buoys to mark boundaries for activities

Orientation Games

Novice paddlers need introductory information about equipment, safety, boat carries, and boat entries and exits, although younger boaters require less detail than older ones. Certainly the method of delivery should be lively to keep everyone interested. Even a simple activity like letting paddlers name their boats and decorate them with colored tape can be incorporated into an equipment talk.

Here are some adaptations of traditional lessons

to provide background knowledge. Feel free to modify the approaches as needed to suit the age of participants.

Paddling Terminology

Draft—*The distance between the waterline and the bottom of the canoe; the degree to which a canoe rests below the water.*

End lines—*Lines attached to the bow and stern of a canoe.*

Thwart—*A cross piece between gunwales that gives shape to the hull.*

Waterline—*The highest point on the hull where water reaches when the canoe rests in the water.*

Scavenger Hunt

Develop a Scavenger Hunt list for boat and paddle parts as well as personal clothing and safety gear. Give the crowd masking tape and a magic marker so they can write on the tape and stick it on the part. The older the crowd, the higher the challenge of technical vocabulary. Include esoteric paddling terms (abundant in the sport!), and let them make educated guesses.

Suggestions:

* Amidships-the middle of the boat.
* Beam-the widest part of the boat
* Bow-the front end of a boat
* Stern-the rear end of a boat
* Freeboard-the degree to which a canoe sits above the water; the distance between the waterline and the gunwales.
* Gunwales-the rails along the edges of the hull.
* Hull-the main body of the boat stripped of any additional parts.

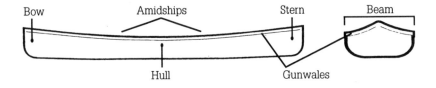

Bow   Amidships   Stern   Beam

Hull   Gunwales

Name It and Claim It

As a great icebreaker for new groups, Name It and Claim It gets people loosened up. Each small group creates a circle with a paddle in the center. As you call out a paddle part, one member must run into the center, pick up the paddle, and "claim" the part by grabbing it (tip, powerface, backface, drip ring, throat, shaft, and so on). Keep calling out parts, until everyone is clustered around holding their piece of the paddle.

With larger groups, two at a time can run to grab the part, which creates a real mob cluster by the end. This game is also appropriate for learning canoe and kayak parts.

Terminology Cards

Develop a common vocabulary by using Terminology Cards which define boat and paddle parts by name. Like flash cards, put the term on one side, definition on the other. (Laminate cards to protect them.) Divide into partners and ask each one in the pair to teach half the material to the other.

Individual and Group Preparedness

Dress-for-the-Weather Box

Fill a box with clothing, paddling gear, life jackets, and wetsuits. Divide into small groups, and give each group a different weather condition. Group members advise their model in the selection and wearing of appropriate clothing. Include some goofy items from your Halloween box just to spice it up!

Observation Game

Cover safety gear with a tarp in preparation for a test of observational skills. Provide each small group with pens and scrap paper, and then give them a 15-second peek under the tarp (a longer look is needed with lots of stuff). Initially ask each individual to list as much as he or she can remember, and then let each small group combine answers for a total group tally. Include first aid kit contents, sunscreen, water bottles, rescue gear, and river maps or guide books.

River Preparation

River Scavenger Hunt

Even flatwater paddlers encounter river sections with current, so an orientation to river features can be useful. Find a small stream, and treat it like a miniature river. Use a scavenger list strategy for small teams to find basic features. Here are some suggestions:

- Black eddy-quiet spot just downstream of a rock or obstacle, with dark water.
- White eddy-a foamy, aerated backflow of water downstream of a rock or obstacle.
- Downstream V-a channel between two obstructions where funneled water meets in a point that creates a V.
- Shoal-a shallow sandy or rocky section of a riverbed away from the main current.
- Strainer-a fallen tree or other obstacle that lets the river flow through but will stop a boat.

River Feature Flash Cards

Create cards with the term on one side and the definition on the other. Divide into small groups, and let the team members use the descriptions to find features in the river. Add pictures to the cards to make the game easier, if general knowledge is low.

Mini Rivers on Land

Build Mini Rivers in small teams by using natural obstacles like rocks, branches, sand and gravel shoals or by using chalk on a driveway. Use small foam boats or paper cut-outs to negotiate the "currents" amid the obstacles and debate strategies for maneuvers. Both kids and adults respond well to the challenge of decision making.

For tandem canoe programs, give two partners a boat, have each team create its own river, and encourage them to discuss strategies, strokes, and communication. This early practice can eliminate later frustration with teamwork when they encounter current. Keep rotating the groups so they "paddle" new rivers.

*   *   *

Do I always address this information? No. I often find that some of this technical material, often so necessary to adults to learn a sport, is unimportant to many younger beginners.

Above all, if any participants are restless to get on water, I get them there quickly and field subsequent questions that arise from their personal experience. There's no substitute for putting a blade to water!

But these activities can be fun filler for rainy days at summer camp and in recreational programs where novices return for several weeks. As "instructor assistants," the more experienced can use the flash cards to help the less skilled gain new knowledge. You'll develop a sense of when participants will be receptive to dry-land activities and information and when the best playground is the water itself.

Calm Water Games

These calm water activities offer the leader two strategies: 1) *building* specific skills as part of guided practice, where the instructor provides immediate feedback, and 2) *reinforcing* skills through more independent practice, where the action is wilder and more complex.

Remember that personality and age can affect responses to these games. A very silly task that thrills a group of eight-year-olds may embarass adolescents. Change the name, the rules, and your delivery to suit the audience. I guarantee that you'll find young and old embracing the spirit of the activities.

Catch Your Neighbor

Craft: kayak & canoe

Line up the boats so they are parallel with 10 feet between each one. Get the group moving slowly sideways in the same direction, and periodically call a change to switch directions. Paddlers must adjust the power of their strokes as needed to remain parallel to other boats at all times.

Begin to call faster and faster changes to speed up the action, and then yell out "catch your neighbor." Occupants in all boats try to overtake and touch their neighbor's boat by bumping it. The game will end as boats bump together. The objective is controlled sideslipping and quick reflex development.

You can easily line up seven or eight boats. As group size increases, create two lines of boat in a front and back row. They play the game within their row.

Spin City

Craft: best in tandem canoes

Begin with the canoes at least two boat lengths apart. Ask each canoe to spin 360 degrees in place and count their number of strokes. Then each boat repeats the 360, trying to reduce the number of strokes to complete the spin. Keep repeating the spin until the fewest number of strokes is reached.

The activity encourages synchronized stroking and efficient use of momentum. It encourages paddlers to "ride the glide" and begin their next stroke just before spin speed ebbs. Ask them which number of strokes created the smoothest spin. (It won't be the lowest number!)

Crab Walk

Craft: tandem canoe

This activity can be a command issued at will throughout a river trip. When a leader calls out "crab," every team must switch places in the boat by one person at a time crab-walking along the gunwales or in the bottom of the canoe. One partner crouches on the bottom, while the other slides hands and feet along the gunwales to reach the new seat. Then the crouched partner moves to the other seat. The goal is keeping the canoe balanced (and upright!) while switching places quickly.

In a race format, establish a start and finish line. Line up the canoes on the start line with at least fifteen feet between each one. Alert them to the likelihood of boats bumping together during the race. After you yell "3-2-1, Go," paddlers paddle five strokes, change positions, and repeat the sequence until they reach the finish line.

An interesting variation is switching positions

Safety Tip: Boats may tip over, so ask that paddlers veer away from overturned boats.

by sitting upright on opposite gunwales, facing the boat's interior. Partners slide their butts along the gunwales, lifting their legs over thwarts, until they reach their new seat. It requires good teamwork between partners to move at the same speed. At amidships, you should be facing each other, before you continue sliding to the new position.

High-Low Bracing
Craft: tandem canoe

High Brace—the paddle is fully inserted and vertical to the water surface with the power face of the paddle toward the boat.

Either paddler can execute a dramatic low brace, and the opposite partner has to save the boat from capsizing with a high brace. The stern paddler has the advantage of seeing the bow. Eventually, play with closed eyes.

This game usually leads into a canoe-over-canoe or T rescue. To perform a T Rescue, position the overturned boat so that it is perpendicular to the upright (rescue) boat. The overturned boat is lifted across the rescue boat to empty the water from it.

Low Brace—the paddle functions like an outrigger, where the shaft is horizontal to the water surface and perpendicular to the boat's centerline with the back face of the blade against the water surface.

Crazy Catamarans and Troubled Trimarans
Craft: kayak or canoe

Pair or triple up boats, and provide fewer paddles than paddlers. Ask the teams to negotiate a different zigzag course around buoys. Use a short course of three or four buoys, because the linked boats are heavy to propel forward. The boats must touch at all times (inventive methods determined by the paddlers!)

Paddles can be passed around between partners. A zigzag course usually means that every person will need a paddle at some time to turn the clump of boats. Every time the team breaks apart, it gets a point. (Of course, they may want to break apart and take a point to change positions!) Fewest points win! Communication is essential, and strong power and turning strokes are developed.

Obstacle Courses

Craft: kayak or canoe

Natural features and inexpensive buoys can create a wealth of obstacle courses. You can time the paddlers on first and second runs, encouraging them to try for a "Personal Best." Provide technical feedback on how they can improve their efficiency. Endless variations can maintain interest and challenge:

- Paddle the course backwards
- One canoe partner is blindfolded; the other is the Seeing Eye
- Pairs of kayakers work as a blindfolded-Seeing Eye team
- Bow paddler sits backward on the seat, facing the stern paddler
- Three or four people paddle a canoe (variation: use kayak paddles)
- Kayaker gives someone a ride on the back deck
- Each craft carries an object on the front kayak deck; start over when it falls off
- Vary the tasks within the course. For example, have paddlers perform two 360-degree turns around buoys before finishing, or sprint around the middle three buoys.

Tug of War

Craft: kayak or canoe

Short-lived, but great fun! Use a 20-foot line to tie together the bows of two boats. Mark the mid-point with brightly colored flagging. Set up the team by a single buoy with the flagging over the buoy. On "Go," paddlers backpaddle and try to pull their opponent past the buoy. Now tie the sterns together

Safety Tip:
Monitor any game carefully when paddlers capsize near ropes.

and repeat. Try to match up the strength of the paired boats, so it's a fair contest.

Shipwreck

Craft: kayak or canoe

Establish a rectangular playing field with four buoys at the corners—about 25 yards by 50 yards for a group of 10 boats. Treat the rectangle as the ship, and identify the edges as bow, stern, port, and starboard. Make sure any side of rectangle is at least 25 feet from shore. Paddlers usually cross the line with a lot of momentum and need a run-out. A leader calls out a direction like "port", and all boats go quickly across that side. Last person to cross becomes the next caller.

Intermingle these commands with some specialty calls that must be performed in the middle of the playing field, such as: "person overboard" (roll); "buddy system" (two boats create a catamaran); "jellyfish" (everybody exits their boat and quickly re-enters); "crow's nest" (two players back to back in a canoe, using their hands as a telescope; in a kayak, create a catamaran facing in opposite directions); "torpedo" (boats spin around); or "island ahead" (everybody rafts up). Last person or team to complete the move makes the next call.

Use only a few simple calls with younger children. This game emphasizes sprinting forward and lots of quick turning.

Safety Tip: Freeze the action if boats risk ramming into each other during the specialty calls. The boats must have clear space before performing these moves.

Everybody's "It"

Craft: canoe or kayak

One paddler is "It" to begin the game. Whenever "It" tags another boat by throwing a wet sponge, the boat also becomes "It." (Leave a lot of bright sponges or balls in the playing area.) It's hard to keep track of how many boats are "it," which is the object of the game. Eventually everybody is tagged except for one craft, which becomes "It" to begin the next game. Establish wider boundaries with skilled paddlers, because the action can be fast. Again, quick sprinting and turning is emphasized.

Keepaway
Craft: canoe or kayak
The object is to avoid a "poison" prop like a ball or sponge (closed plastic food containers work in a pinch) that a player tries to lob into or onto another boat. If the poison prop touches your kayak, you are "It." The prop needs to land in your canoe. I've watched groups play this game for an entire day, as the "poison" boat tries to sneak up on other craft and hit them unexpectedly with the ball. This game can keep kids moving ahead on a river trip.

FreeStyle Boat Dancing
Craft: kayak or canoe
Each player selects a two- to three-minute song; he or she must then create a dance of flowing paddling maneuvers to that music. Teams of boats can also work together to create a choreographed number set to music. You provide the tape or CD player; they'll bring their favorite, often wild tapes or CDs! A panel of judges can establish criteria and award Olympic-style points for each performance. This works well for a multi-day program, where participants can work on their routines at their leisure over several days in preparation for a final exhibition for the entire group or the whole camp.

Tape or Tail Tag
Craft: kayak or canoe
Stick a six-inch length of duct tape on the end of each boat. This is the boat's tail. Designate boundaries to

keep boats in a small area. The object is simple: try to grab as many pieces of tape as possible while trying to keep other paddlers from grabbing your taped tail. Paddlers can grab only the tape, not any part of the boat.

Reverse Sweeping Low Brace—

a moving version of the low brace, which braces and turns the canoe; the back face of the paddle blade is pressed against the water surface and sweeps forward in a 180-degree arc (for this exercise).

J Stroke—

a corrective stroke to keep a canoe on a straight course; the paddler carves a J or backward J through the water with the paddle vertical to the water surface.

Low-Brace 360s

Craft: canoe

Change a slow, elegant reverse sweeping low brace into a J stroke into another sweep brace to execute continuous 360's. In a tandem canoe, both paddlers perform the sweep braces on the same side and synchronize the sequence of strokes. Go for extreme boat lean, and dip the gunwale into the water. Teamwork is essential!

Whirlygig

Craft: kayak

A swimmer clings to the rear deck of the kayak, and the kayaker tries to dislodge the person with fast and abrupt moves and by rolling the boat. Goal: see how long it takes the swimmer to let go.

Otter Entries

Craft: kayak

Make sure the flotation bags are fully inflated for this game. The players paddle about 50 feet from shore, flip over, swim out of their boat, and lodge their paddle in the boat. Yell "3-2-1-Go," and players swim from shore to the kayaks, dislodge the paddles, and dive under the kayak to insert their bodies upside down into the craft. Roll up.

Follow-the-Leader Mirror Ballet

Craft: kayak or canoe

Pair up the boats, and ask players to perform this exercise without talking. The lead boater chooses a ballet routine of different moves and begins to perform them. Then the following partner attempts to mimic the same moves as simultaneously as possible on flatwater in a side-by-side formation. The emphasis is flowing transitions between moves, rather than speed or paddling long distances. Try the activity at a moving water practice site, too, where students try to stay as close as possible in a follow-the-leader pattern.

Wet Sponge Polo

Craft: kayak or canoes
Establish a rectangular playing field 25 by 50 yards with two goals at each end (anchored plastic laundry baskets on floats work well; so do two plastic jug buoys). Divide into two teams; as few as two or three boats on a team will work, but reduce the field size unless you want them to have a good workout.

Each team tries to score goals against the other by throwing a dead fish (really, a wet sponge) into the basket. Establish some clear rules, such as: Pass the sponge from paddle to paddle (or hand to hand); possession goes to the other team when the sponge is dropped; ramming of another boat results in a foul and a shot on goal. You make them up. The younger the group, the simpler the rules. A nice variation is hand paddling by kayakers or standing up in canoes.

Kaleidoscope

Craft: kayak and maneuverable canoes
Some people don't remember Jackie Gleason's June Taylor Dancers, but this activity reminds me of an overhead camera recording a kaleidoscope of dance action. All boats begin in a pinwheel with bows pointing into the center. Then a dance leader begins to call out various moves: Spin the pinwheel left, spin it right, back out, complete a 180, back into the circle. All boats needs to match their speed to create synchronized "dancing," which creates group awareness.

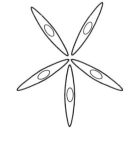

Catamaran Tag

Craft: kayak or canoes

Establish boundaries according to abilities: The better the paddlers, the larger the playing area. Elect an "It," who paddles around trying to tag another boat with a soft ball. Boats can join together in a catamaran to be "safe" from being tagged. However, they can touch in a catamaran for a maximum of only five seconds. If another paddler comes alongside and hooks up with the paired group, then the outside member of the original pair must break away. With larger groups, use two or more balls to increase the intensity.

Safety Tip:
Participants must be aware of other players' hands and paddles when they create a catamaran.

Rolling

Beyond hand rolls, many other variations exist for the individual. Count the total number of non-stop rolls, rolls in one minute, and rolls with one breath. Encourage paddlers to establish "Personal Bests" rather than compete against each other. Try these variations:

Slowest roll: Who can take the longest time to roll while continuously moving? Synchronized rolling: Start with pairs, keep adding paddlers to a group. Wave of rolls in a line: By the time the paddler at the end of the line is finished, the first person has already begun rolling again. The "wave" rolls on....

Give Me

Craft: kayak or canoe

Establish a starting line on the beach and a finish line about 25 yards across the water, where the caller waits in a boat. Divide the group into small teams (three to four boats in each team promotes more activity), spaced evenly across the beach, and give each team a box of props.

The object is to give the leader what he or she

asks by performing the task and paddling past the caller (rather than converging on the person!) Examples of "give me's": two people wearing frisbees on their heads; a person in pink following a person wearing a hat; four people in a canoe; four paddling in unison; everyone wearing another person's lifejacket; two people towing another person, and so on. The tasks should require quick thinking, team work, and creativity.

The first team across the line gets a point, but the crazier you make the tasks, the less people will keep count.

Scavenger Hunts

Craft: canoe or kayak

Give paddlers a list of objects or features that they need to find. Establish guidelines for the action, like they can use only the summer camp property or they must stay within a cove. Establish a finish time, and let them go. Small teams work well in encouraging strategy development. It allows a group to send less skilled teammates to closer locations and better skilled teammates across longer distances.

You can mix different themes with paddling: nature and environmental education, sensory awareness, or just outlandish fun. I've seen camp programs where nature guidebooks are left on the beach for reference, and people paddle to islands or points of land to find items. Players should be oriented to low-impact outdoor guidelines where they collect only dead or inert items (and mark on a map where they found a live item).

Paddle Orienteering

Craft: kayak or canoe

Use USGS topographical maps for your lake or river section, or conduct a mapmaking session where

Scavenger Items

maple leaf• hemlock needles• granite rock• three different seeds• a thorn

•

something sharp• something straight• a bright object• a noisy item• two different textures• a sweet smell

•

weird t-shirt• candy wrapper• purple socks• something beautiful• something broken• something like yourself young paddlers draw the features of a cove or lake on a simple map. I've worked with 5th-graders who can read topo maps quite well.

The best site has an island or two, a ragged shoreline, or constructed obstacles like docks and rafts. Ask the participants to copy "control" points off your master map where you have hidden an object(s) that they must find. I have used buttons, candy, stickers, symbols on cardboard, orange flagging, unusual items (orange buoy under a bush), and real orienteering punches (where they must punch the side of their maps to prove they reached the destination). Set a time limit based on paddling abilities and the number of controls.

An interesting variation is score orienteering. Here you divide the group into teams who will try to find the controls. Assign point values to the controls (closest ones get 5 points, farthest get 25 points), and let each team decide who they'll send to the various places. Give them a time limit, perhaps a half hour or an hour, to see how many total objects (and points) they can bring back.

Red Light, Green Light
Craft: kayak or canoe

The person who is "It" faces away from a group lined up on a starting line. "It" calls "green light" to get players moving and calls "red light" to stop the action. The caller spins around, opens his or her eyes, and sends moving players back to the starting line. You may have to ask the caller to wait three seconds before looking to give paddlers a chance to stop. First paddler to reach "It" is now "It."

Mirror Image
Craft: kayak or canoe

Pair up. Ask them to mimic their partner's paddling style through a sequence of maneuvers. Ask them to discuss how they change their own style. Switch roles, and repeat. Participants can discover new, effective ways of paddling by following someone else's timing, strategies, or technical model.

Raft En Masse (Mess)

Craft: kayak or canoe

All boats raft up in a line. Paddlers prepare to hold hands, and stand up at the same time—a very hard task in kayaks and tippier canoes. Kayakers can prepare for the group challenge by first practicing alone or in small groups of three. Again, the fun factor is higher than the paddling value, but this balance exercise leads into learning wet entries into boats without going to shore.

Moving Water Games

Practice in milder current is important for allowing students to develop good form while getting used to river hydrology. A good practice site has the following characteristics:

- Eddies (at least two large ones) with clearly-defined eddy lines
- Obstacles to enhance river awareness
- Easy rescue area

Current that allows paddlers to paddle back upriver is another characteristic. Use a site with just enough current to require good boat lean in entering and exiting eddies.

Peelout—*the paddler follows a U-shaped path in exiting the eddy facing upriver and turning downriver*

Eddy turn—*the paddler follows a U-shaped path in entering the eddy, so he or she faces upriver behind the obstacle at the end of the turn.*

Ferry—*a more lateral move across the river, where the boat is angled against the current and the boater paddles to prevent excessive downriver slippage.*

Turns in Sequence

Craft: kayak and canoe

Begin with the C turn, which requires a peelout to an eddy turn from the same eddy. The S-turn sequence—a peelout to an eddy turn—can be followed by a ferry back to the initial eddy. Use these tasks with both sequences:

- Hand paddle the sequence to feel the river currents
- Count the total number of strokes in the sequence; keep reducing the total number to see how few are needed
- Use paddle strokes only for momentum; execute all turns with boat lean only
- Paddle in reverse

Building Blocks

Craft: kayak or canoe

A group of five or six kids can build a sequence of moves in follow-the-leader fashion. The first one chooses a maneuver near the top of the practice site, and everyone performs it. Then the second chooses a second maneuver, and the group links two moves together. After each individual in turn adds a move before another practice round, the group will end up with a final 5- or 6-move sequence. The add-on approach helps to build more and more flowing moves over longer distances. This activity can also be used on calm water.

Gossip

Craft: kayak or canoe

An adult leader or one skilled paddler in the group identifies a sequence of moves for practice. Each player executes the sequence. The leader or paddler identifies a necessary technical correction and whispers it to the next player who sends the message down the line like the old gossip game.

The leader should check the message at the end of the line to see if it's accurate. Then the group practices the new focus. The Voyageur Program uses this exercise to encourage kids to transmit technical information, and it works well with junior high groups. Repeat with a new leader and sequence of moves. This activity can also be used on calm water.

Gate Reduction

Craft: kayak or canoe

At a practice site with gates (poles hung from wires), identify a short 5-gate sequence. Time each participant's completion of the sequence to establish a base time. They each have two tries to reduce their time. If they don't, they get a point. Provide feedback to help them improve their paddling efficiency or river strategies. Use five-second penalties for hitting a gate and fifty seconds for missing a gate entirely. Create another 5-gate sequence of moves to continue the game.

Gate Reduction is similar to Building Blocks in that they develop short sequences of moves, but the emphasis here is speed and efficiency, not necessarily flowing moves. Use Building Blocks first as a warm-up.

Rescue

All newcomers need to make sure their practice of rescue techniques keeps pace with their paddling skills. While some adults, particularly non-swimmers, may be apprehensive about tipping over boats, kids often love to capsize and they can thoroughly enjoy rescue practices.

All paddlers need to be acquainted with their responsiblity to themselves—rescue actively. These games encourage direct personal action for such rescues in canoes and kayaks. The activities in this section are deliberately less playful to enhance safety during practice.

Towing on Flatwater
Flip over, and swim quickly with the boat and paddle gear to a nearby marker. (Use a short distance like 10 yards for canoes!) Note the elapsed time, and repeat to achieve a Personal Best time.

Swamped Canoe or Kayak Races
Establish a start and finish line on flatwater. Paddlers must capsize at a certain point marked by a buoy, roll over their swamped boat, re-enter the craft, and paddle the wallowing whale to shore.

Beat the Clock
Variations of a basic T or canoe over canoe rescue can provide extended, enjoyable practice. The T rescue relies on a paddler in an upright craft pulling an overturned boat across the bow (in a solo canoe or kayak) or across amidships (in a tandem canoe) to empty it. The newly-emptied craft is then held alongside the rescue craft to create a stable platform for re-entering.

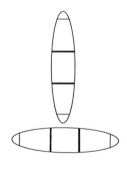

Time the first rescue and then compare the times of each successive rescue to show improvement. Emphasize smooth and cooperative rescues because trying to beat the clock can encourage some flailing. Now perform the rescue silently.

Coordinated teams of kids can actually rescue a swamped canoe in less than a minute after initial practice. Here are some variations to spice up practice.

Canoe Log Roll

Designate one swimmer as a "helpless swimmer" in a canoe T rescue, and let the rescue team figure out how to care for and get a limp person into the rescued canoe. Rolling the victim like a log over the gunwale works well; scooping in a heavier victim may be necessary by lowering the gunwale. Time these efforts; let the swimmer share how the rescue felt.

Kayak Scoop

Designate one person as the "injured" swimmer in a kayak T rescue, and let the rescuer use a scoop rescue to get the swimmer back into the cockpit. A third kayaker can be very helpful in lifting the victim's torso as the partner is righting the kayak. Like the canoe scoop, this rescue is effective with paddlers with disabilities.

Self Rescues in Current

All activities here must be preceded by a review of safety principles involved in swimming in current and by initial swimming practice. Site selection is important; a river section with few obstacles and big eddies at the bottom of a mild rapid is best for initial practice. Always closely supervise rescue practice to enhance safety.

These exercises rely on the basic river swimming position, where people float on their backs with their heads upriver and feet downriver near the surface to fend off obstacles.

Link elbows with a partner and sidestroke to shore as one unit (nice for the nervous). Close your eyes and feel the currents as you sidestroke to shore in a section with few obstacles. Count how many changes in current you felt. Look upriver, and see if you can find those different lines of current. Catch a ball or rescue bag thrown from shore.

Use your feet to push off a rock and quickly spin around 360 degrees so you're facing downstream again. See how many pirouettes you can perform. It's great practice for regaining the swimming position.

Mock Tow Rescues

This activity allows initial practice of tow rescues without capsizing boats, so paddlers learn how to maneuver into the proper position for a tow. One boat, still upright, begins to drift and calls for a rescue. The rescue boat swoops into a ferry position above the "stranded" boat. A rescuer hands the stern end line to the "victim" in the upstream end of the canoe. The rescue boat paddles the stranded boat directly to shore. Progress to real capsizes, once the rescue boats are able to get into the proper rescue position.

Conclusion

As a novice paddler, you have uncovered in this book some interesting ways to develop skills. Let them get you excited about paddling and stimulate your learning.

As an instructor or parent, you may be searching for new ways to keep students or kids enthusiastic about paddling. This book provides lots of ideas to use and modify; the only limit is your imagination.

You'll find that games speed learning and create a camaraderie that all paddlers can enjoy. My most rewarding moments as a paddling instructor have been when a group has obviously enjoyed the session and doesn't want to stop. Neither do I! They are excited about paddling and are likely to do so again.

That, after all, is the most important goal. Enjoy the water wonderland!

The American Canoe Association
7432 Alban Station Blvd. Suite B-226
Springfield, VA 22150
Ph: 703/451-0141   E-Mail: ACADirect@aol.com

The American Canoe Association
7432 Alban Station Blvd. Suite B-226
Springfield, VA 22150
Ph: 703/451-0141   E-Mail: ACADirect@aol.com

☑ YES! I want to join the American Canoe Association. Enclosed is $25 for the membership.

Name:_____

As an ACA member you get:

Address:_____

City/State/Zip:_____

☑ ACA Membership Card
☑ *Paddler* Magazine
☑ ACA Newsletter
☑ Equipment Discounts
☑ ACA Member Decal
☑ Access to ACA Events

Phone:_____Birth Date:_____

Charge Card Users (Visa, MasterCard or Amex)

Type of Card:_____Card#_____

ExpDate:_____Signature:_____

☑ YES! Send me my free membership in the American Canoe Association so I can join the fun and adventure of canoeing, kayaking and rafting!

DATE OF
NAME:_____BIRTH_____

HOME
ADDRESS:_____

_____

Indicate areas of interest:_____

How did you find out about the ACA?_____

(* Must be between the ages of 11-17 years of age to qualify.)
LIMITED TIME OFFER - RESPOND TODAY!

An Invitation to Adventure!

Free Membership for Young People (11-17 years)

Do you like outdoor sports and adventure? A free membership in the American Canoe Association will introduce you to the fun and excitement of canoeing, kayaking and rafting.

As an ACA member you get:

☑ACA Membership Card
☑ACA Newsletter
☑Access to ACA Events
☑ACA Member Decal
☑Equipment Discounts